Gregor Reisch's sixteenth-century engraving showing Pythagoras using a medieval counting board to form the numbers 1,241 and 82 (right) while Boethius calculates using the Indian numerals we are familiar with today (left). In the centre is Arithmetic, with the two geometric progressions 1,2,4,8, and 1,3,9,27 appearing on her dress.

This edition © Wooden Books Ltd 2009
First published 2005 by Walker & Co, New York

Published by Wooden Books Ltd.
8A Market Place, Glastonbury, Somerset

British Library Cataloguing in Publication Data
Lundy, M.
Sacred Number

A CIP catalogue record for this little book
may be available from the British Library.

ISBN 1 904263 44 5

Printed and bound in Shanghai, China
by Shangahi iPrinting Co., Ltd.

WOODEN
BOOKS

SACRED
NUMBER

THE SECRET QUALITIES OF QUANTITIES

by

Miranda Lundy

with additional illustrations by

Richard Henry, Daud Sutton & Adam Tetlow

to parents, and children

My sincere thanks to Adam Tetlow, Richard Henry, Daud Sutton, and John Martineau for their painstaking assistance in the design and editing of this little book, and also to my many tutors in these profound quantities, particularly Professor Keith Critchlow and John Michell. Additional thanks to Sally Pucill, Haifa Khawaja, and Delfina Bottesini. Thanks particularly to Jim Baldwin for getting the ball rolling.

"The Tao gives birth to the One,
the One gives birth to the Two,
the Two gives birth to the Three,
the Three gives birth to the Ten Thousand Things."
Lao Tzu

CONTENTS

INTRODUCTION

What is number? How do we distinguish the one from the many, or, for that matter, the two from the three? A crow, disturbed by four men going to hide under its tree, can carefully count them home again from a distance, one by one, tired and hungry, before returning safely to its nest. But five ...

We all know certain things about certain numbers: six pops up in snowflakes, there are seven notes in a scale, we count in tens, three legs make a stool, five petals form a flower. Some of these elementary discoveries are actually the first universal truths we ever come across, so simple we forget about them. Children on distant planets are probably having the same experiences.

The science and study of number is one of the oldest on Earth, its origins lost in the mists of time. Early cultures wrote numbers in pottery markings, weaving patterns, notched bones, knots, stone monuments, and the numbers of their gods. Later systems integrated the mysteries under the magical medieval Quadrivium of arithmetic, geometry, music, and astronomy—the four liberal arts required for a true understanding of the quality of number.

All science has its origin in magic, and in the ancient schools no magician was ever unschooled in the power of number. These days the lore of sacred number has been usurped by a tide of merely quantitative numbers, not covered in these pages. This book is a beginner's guide to mystic arithmology, a small attempt to unveil some of the many secret and essential qualities of number contained within Unity.

THE MONAD
one unity

Unity. The One. God. The Great Spirit. Mirror of wonders. The still eternity. Permanence. There are countless names for it.

According to one perspective, one cannot actually speak of the One, because to speak of it is to make an object of it, implying separation from it, so misrepresenting the essence of oneness from the start, a mysterious conundrum.

The One is the limit of all, first before the beginning and last after the end, alpha and omega, the mold that shapes all things and the one thing shaped by all molds, the origin from which the universe emerges, the universe itself, and the centre to which it returns. It is point, seed, and destination.

One is echoed in all things and treats all equally. Its stability among numbers is unique, one remaining one when multiplied or divided by itself, and one of anything is uniquely that one thing. One is alone, all one, and no thing can exist to describe it.

All things are immersed in the shoreless ocean of Unity. The quality of oneness permeates everything, and while there is nothing without it, there is also no thing within it, as even a communication or idea requires parts in relationship. Like light from the sun or gentle rain the One is unconditional in its love, yet its majesty and mystery remain veiled, and beyond apprehension, for the One can only be understood by itself.

One is simultaneously circle, centre, and the purest tone.

DUALITY

opposites

There are two sides to every coin, and the other side is where the Dyad lives. Two is the otherworldly shadow, opposite, polarised, and objectified. It is there, other, that not this, and essential as a basis for comparison, the method by which our minds know things. There are countless names for the divine pair.

To the Pythagoreans, two was the first sexed number, even and female. To develop their appreciation of twoness, they contemplated pairs of pure opposites, such as limited-unlimited, odd-even, one-many, right-left, male-female, resting-moving, and straight-curved. We might also think of the positive and negative charge in electromagnetism, and the in and out of our breathing.

The dyad appears in music as the ratio two to one, as we experience a similar tone an octave higher or lower, at twice or half the pitch. In geometry it is a line, two points, or two circles.

Linguistically when speaking of both parts of something working as one we use the bi- prefix, as in bicycle or binary, but when the divisive quality of two is invoked, words begin with the prefix di-, thus discord or diversion. The distinction between self and not-self is one of the first and last we generally make.

Modern philosophers, if they stop to think about twoness, can get little further than the ancients. All experience a left and a right, front and back, and up and down through two eyes and two ears. Men and women alike live under a Sun and a Moon, sometimes remembering how miraculously balanced they seem, the same size in the sky, one shining by day, the other by night.

THREE
is a crowd

Male in some cultures, female in others, three, like a tree, bridges heaven and earth. The Triad relates opposites as their comixture, solution, or mediator. It is the synthesis or return to unity after the division of two and traditionally the first odd number.

The third leg of a stool gives it balance, the third strand of a braid makes a plait. Stories, fairy tales, and spiritual traditions abound with portentous threes, juggling past, present, and future with the knower, knowing, and the known. As birth, life, and death, the triad appears throughout nature, in principle and form.

Trinity often takes the form of a triangle, the most simple and structurally stable polygon, defining our first surface.

In music the ratios three to two and three to one define the intervals of the fifth and its octave, the most beautiful harmonies other than the octave itself, and the key to ancient tunings.

The *vesica piscis* formed by two overlapping circles (*opposite top left*) immediately invokes triangles. An equilateral triangle in a circle defines the octave, so that the area of the ring (*below left*) is three times that of the small circle. Below centre we see Archimedes' favorite discovery—the volumes of the cone, sphere, and drum are in the ratios one to two to three.

QUATERNITY
two pairs

Beyond three we enter the realm of manifestation. Four is the first born thing, the first product of procreation, two twos. The Tetrad is thus the first square number other than one, and a symbol of the Earth and the natural world.

Four is the basis of three-dimensional space. The simple solid known as the tetrahedron, or "four facer", is made of four triangles, or four points or spheres and is as fundamental to the structure of space as the triangle is to the plane.

Four is often associated with the material modes of mani-festation, Fire, Air, Earth and Water, and a square around a circle defines a heavenly ring whose area is equal to the enclosed circle (*opposite, top right*). The solstices and equinoxes quarter the year, horses walk on four legs, and other earthly fours abound.

Four as static square is echoed by the dynamic cross. The interplay of cross and square is encoded within the traditional rite of orientation for a new building, where the sunrise and sunset shadows from a central pillar give the symbolic east-west axis. The principle of quadrature is universal, appearing in ancient Chinese texts and the writings of Vitruvius. It survives today in the term *quarters*, referring to the districts of a city.

All everyday matter is appropriately made of just four particles: protons, neutrons, electrons, and electron neutrinos.

Four appears in music as the third overtone, four to one, which is two octaves, and also as the ratio four to three, known as the fourth, which is the complement of the fifth inside the octave.

PHIVE
life itself

The quality of five is magical. Children instinctively draw fivefold stars, and we all sense its phizzy, energetic quality.

Five marries male and female—as two and three in some cultures, or three and two in others—and so is the universal number of reproduction and biological life. It is also the number of water, every molecule of which is a corner of a pentagon. Water itself is an amazing liquid crystal lattice of flexing icosahedra, these being one of the five Platonic solids (*below, second from right*), five triangles meeting at each point. As such, water shows its quality as being that of flow, dynamism, and life. Dry things are either dead or they are awaiting water.

Fives are found in apples, flowers, hands, and feet. Our nearest planet, Venus, goddess of love and beauty, draws a lovely fivefold pattern about Earth as she whirls around the sun (*opposite, top left*).

Our most universal scale, the pentatonic, is made of five tones (the black keys on a piano), grouped into two and three. The Renaissance demand for intervals involving the number five, like the major third, which uses the ratio five to four, produced the modern scale. Five is the diagonal of a three-by-four rectangle.

Unlike threes and fours, fives disdain the plane, waiting for the third dimension to fit together to produce the fifth element.

11

ALL THINGS SIXY
the hex

The Hexad like its graceful herald the snowflake, brings perfection, structure, and order. The marriage by multiplication of two and three, even and odd, six is also the number of creation, with a cosmos made in six days a common theme in scripture.

The numbers that easily divide other numbers are known as their factors, and most numbers, including one to five, have factors that sum to less than themselves, and so are known as deficient. Six, beautifully, is the sum and product of the first three numbers, and its factors are also just one, two, and three, these summing to six and so making it the first perfect number.

The radius of a circle can be swung through its circumference in exactly six identical arcs to inscribe a regular hexagon, and six circles perfectly fit around one. After the triangle and square the hexagon is the final regular polygon that can tile perfectly with identical copies of itself to fill the plane.

The three dimensions make for six directions: forward, backward, left, right, up, and down, and these are embodied in the six faces of a cube, the six corners of an octahedron and the six edges of a tetrahedron. Six occurs widely in crystalline structures such as snowflakes, quartz, and graphite, and hexagons of carbon atoms form the basis of organic chemistry. Just add water.

Curiously, the well-known Pythagorean three, four, five triangle has an area and a semiperimeter of six.

Insects creep and crawl on six legs, and the honey bee arranges its dry, waxy secretions into an instinctive hexagonal honeycomb.

THE HEPTAD

seven sisters

Seven is the Virgin, standing quite alone and having little to do with any of the other simple numbers. In music a scale of seven tones emerges as naturally as its sister five-tone scale. These are the white keys on the piano, producing the seven modes of antiquity, a universal pattern. Like all numbers, seven embodies the number preceeding it; spatially it functions as the spiritual centre of six, as six directions emanate from a point in space, and six working circles surround a seventh restful one in a plane.

The Moon's phases are widely counted in four sevens with a mysterious moonless night or two completing its true cycle.

Our eyes perceive three primary colours of light—red, green and blue—which combine to produce four more—yellow, cyan, magenta and white. According to the ancient Indians, a vertical rainbow of seven subtle energy centres, or 'chakras', runs up our bodies. Today we understand these as the seven endocrine glands.

The seven planets of antiquity, arranged in order of their speed (*opposite upper centre*), make amazing connections with their metals (*opposite upper left*) and the days of the week (*opposite upper right*): Moon- ☽ -silver-Monday, Mercury- ☿ -quicksilver-Wednesday, Venus- ♀ -copper-Friday, Sun- ☉ -gold-Sunday, Mars- ♂ -iron-Tuesday, Jupiter- ♃ -tin-Thursday, and Saturn- ♄ -lead-Saturday.

There are seven frieze symmetries, seven groups of crystal structures, and seven coils in the traditional labyrinth (*all shown opposite*).

EIGHT
a pair of squares

Eight is two times two times two, and as such is the first cubic number after one. As the number of vertices of a cube or faces of its dual, the octahedron, eight is complete. At the molecular level this is displayed by atoms, which long to have a full octave of eight electrons in their outermost shell. A sulfur atom has six electrons in its outermost shell, so eight atoms get together to share electrons, forming an octagonal sulphur ring.

Within architecture the octagon often signifies the transition between Heaven and Earth, as a bridge between the square and the circle. A spherical dome often surmounts a cubic structure by way of a beautiful octagonal vault.

Eight is particularly revered in the religion and mythology of the orient. The ancient Chinese oracle, the *I-Ching*, is based on combinations of eight trigrams, each the result of a twofold choice made three times. Depicted opposite is the "Former Heaven Sequence", said to represent the ideal pattern of transformations in the cosmos. Note how each trigram is the complement of its opposite.

In religious symbolism, the eighth step is often associated with spiritual evolution or salvation. This may result from the fact that in a seven-tone scale the eighth note is the octave, twice the pitch of the first note, and so signals the movement to a new level.

In the modern world, computers think in delightful units called "bytes", each made of eight binary "bits".

All spiders have eight legs and all octopi have eight tentacles.

THE ENNEAD
three threes

Cats have nine lives, dress to the nines whenever possible, and seem to spend most of their time on cloud nine, wherever that is.

Nine is the triad of triads, the first odd square number, and with it something extraordinary occurs, for the first nine numbers can be arranged in a magic square where every line of three in any direction has the same total (*opposite, centre*). This ancient number pattern was first spotted four millennia ago on the shell of a divine turtle emerging from the river Lo in China.

Three times three is one more than two times two times two, and the ratio between nine and eight defines the crucial whole tone in music, the seed from which the scale emerges, as the difference between the two most simple harmonies in the octave, the fifth (three to two), and the fourth (four to three).

There are nine regular three-dimensional shapes: the five Platonic solids and the four stellar Kepler-Poinsot polyhedra.

Nine appears in our bodies as the cross-section of the tentacle-like cilia, which move things around our surfaces, and the bundles of microtubes in centrioles, essential for cell division (*below*).

Nine is the celestial number of order, and many ancient traditions speak of nine worlds, or spheres.

TEN
fingers and thumbs

The fact that humans have eight fingers plus two thumbs must have worked in ten's favour, as cultures as various as the Incas, the Indians, the Berbers, the Hittites, and the Minoans all adopted it as the base for their counting systems. Today we all use base ten. Ten is the child of five and two, and unsurprisingly the word *ten* derives from the Indo-European *dekm*, meaning "two hands".

Ten is particularly formed as the sum of the first four numbers, one plus two plus three plus four, a fact of profound significance to the Pythagoreans who immortalized it in the figure of the Tetraktys (*black dots, opposite centre*) and called it Universe, Heaven, and Eternity. As well as being the fourth triangular number, ten is also the third tetrahedral number (*opposite lower right*), a fact that lends it great importance as a simultaneous building number of both two- and three-dimensional triangular form.

Ten life-invoking pentagons sit perfectly around a decagon, and DNA, appropriately as the key to the reproduction of life, has ten steps for each turn of its double helix, so appears in cross-section as a tenfold rosette (*opposite, top left*).

There are ten sephiroth in the Jewish Kabbalah's Tree of Life (*opposite lower left*) and tenfold symmetry was often used in Gothic architecture (*opposite, top right*).

Plato believed that the decad contained all numbers, and for most of us today it does, as we can express just about any number we care to in terms of just ten simple symbols.

ELEVENSES
measure and the moon

Eleven is a mysterious underworldly number. In German it goes by the appropriate name of *Elf*. It is important as the first number that allows us to begin to comprehend the measure of a circle. This is because, for practical purposes, a circle measuring seven across will measure eleven halfway round (*opposite, top left*).

This relationship between eleven and seven was considered so profound by the ancient Egyptians that they used it as the basis for the design of the Great Pyramid. A circle drawn around the elevation of the Great Pyramid has the same perimeter as that of its square base. The intended seven-elevenfold conversion between square and curve is demonstrated by numerous surveys.

The ancients were obsessed with measures, and the number eleven is central in their metrological scheme. Shown opposite is the extraordinary fact that the size of the Moon relates to the size of the Earth as does three to eleven. What this means is that if we draw down the Moon to the Earth, as shown, then a heavenly circle through the Moon will have a circumference equal to the perimeter of a square around the Earth. This is called "squaring the circle". Quite how the old druids worked this out we may never know, but they clearly did, for the Moon and the Earth are best measured in miles, as shown.

Eleven, seven, and three are all Lucas numbers, sisters of the Fibonacci numbers, new numbers forming from the sum of the previous two numbers. The Fibonacci sequence begins 1, 1, 2, 3, 5, 8, whereas the Lucas sequence begins 1, 3, 4, 7, 11.

*moon
and earth
sizes 3 : 11*

*moon diameter
= 3 x 1 x 2 x 3 x 4 x 5 x 6
= 3 x 8 x 9 x 10   miles*

*earth diameter
= 11 x 1 x 2 x 3 x 4 x 5 x 6
= 8 x 9 x 10 x 11   miles*

*moon
and earth
(large circle)*

*combined radius
= 1 x 2 x 3 x 4 x 5 x 6 x 7
= 7 x 8 x 9 x 10   miles*

*area of heavenly circle = twice
1 x 2 x 3 x 4 x 5 x 6 x 7 x 8 x 9 x 10 x 11
square miles*

THE TWELVE
heaven and earth

Twelve is the first abundant number, with factors one, two, three, four, and six, summing to more than itself. Twelve points on a circle can join to form four triangles, three squares, or two hexagons (*centre opposite*). As the product of three and four, twelve is also often associated with their sum seven.

Twelve enjoys the third dimension and is the number of edges of both the cube and the octahedron. The icosahedron has twelve vertices, and its dual, the dodecahedron (literally "twelve facer") has twelve faces of regular pentagons. Twelve spheres fit perfectly around one to define a cuboctahedron.

In a seven-note scale, notes increase as a pattern of five whole tones and two semitones. In modern tuning the five whole tones are divided to create a scale of twelve identical semitones, the well-tempered twelve-tone scale we all hear every day.

Curiously, the next most simple Pythagorean triangle, after the three-four-five, has sides of five, twelve, and thirteen.

Twelve is often found arranged around a central solar hero, and there are many twelve-tribe nations. In ancient China, Egypt, and Greece, cities were often divided into twelve sections, and, of course, there are usually twelve full moons in a year.

The material universe is today understood as being made of three generations of four fundamental particles, twelve in all.

24

COVENS AND SCORES
into higher numbers

Alas, in a such a tiny book as this there is not enough space to cover every number in detail, so we will skip on. Small entries on higher numbers appear in the glossary (*see pages 56 and 57*).

Thirteen, the coven, beloved of the ancient Maya, and central to the structure of a deck of cards, is a Fibonacci number expressed in the motions of Venus, for whom thirteen years is eight of our own, and lest you think it unlucky, remember the teacher of twelve disciples is the thirteenth member of the gang, as the thirteenth tone in the chromatic scale completes the octave.

Fourteen, as twice seven, and fifteen, as three fives, each have unique qualities but begin to demonstrate how non prime higher numbers tend to be perceived in terms of their factors.

Sixteen is $2 \times 2 \times 2 \times 2$, the square of four (itself a square).

Seventeen keeps many secrets. Both Japanese haiku and Greek hexameter consist of seventeen syllables, and Islamic mystics often refer to it as particularly beautiful.

Eighteen, as twice nine and thrice six, and nineteen, a prime number, both have strong connections to the moon (*see page 32*).

Twenty, a score, the sum of fingers and toes, is a base in many cultures. Finger-counting, as in the example shown (*opposite*), was widespread in medieval European markets. In French eighty is still *quatre-vingt* (four twenties) and the ancient Maya used a sophisticated base-20 system (*glyphs for 1-19 shown below*).

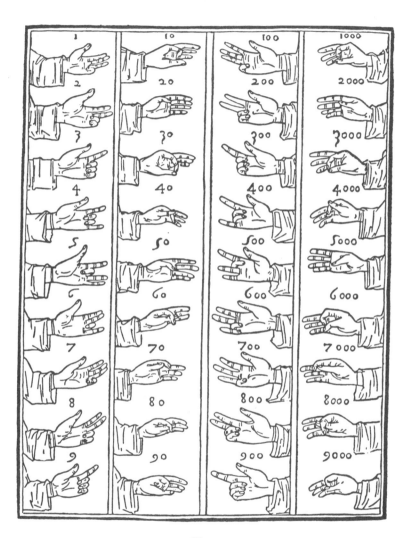

THE QUADRIVIUM
four liberal arts

How do we get a feel for numbers other than by their quantities? What are their qualities? One traditional method is by way of the seven liberal arts. Three of these, the Trivium of logic, rhetoric, and grammar, cover the gift of the gab, including poetry, while the remaining four, the Quadrivium, investigate number itself, geometry (number in space), music (number in time), and cosmology (number in space and time).

Number itself, outside space and time, forms the subject of the study of factors, prime or perfect numbers, and numbers like those found in the Fibonacci and Lucas sequences (*see page 58*).

The numbers of space are a distinct and fascinating bunch. How does space carve up? Opposite we see some of the limits placed by space on number. There are three regular grids (*top left*), five regular solids (*top right*), eight semi-regular grids (*centre left*) and thirteen semi-regular solids (*centre right*). Each of these helps to color the qualities of the numbers they invoke.

The numbers of music (*lower opposite*) begin their amazing journey as the most simple ratios possible, 1:1 (unison), 2:1 (the octave), 3:2 (the fifth), and 4:3 (the fourth). The frequency of the fifth differs from that of the fourth as 9:8 (the wholetone). Thus the numbers of music unfold as the spaces between fractions.

These numerical facts of space and time are universal. They may or may not play the same tunes in the nearest intelligent galaxy, but they will agree that fifths and octaves sound good, and they will probably recognise the five simple regular solids.

GNOMONS
ways of growing

Aristotle observed that some things suffer no change other than magnitude when they grow. He was describing the principle the Greeks referred to as "gnomonic growth". Originally a term for a carpenter's tool, a gnomon is defined as any figure, which, when added to another figure, leaves the resultant figure similar to the original. The contemplation of the gnomon leads to an understanding of one of nature's most common principles, growth by accretion. The more permanent bodily tissues, such as bones, teeth, horns, and shells all develop in this way.

The ancients had a general fascination with patterns and progressions created by whole-number ratios. Examples are Plato's Lambdoma, which produces the full range of musical ratios, and the proportional rectangles used in Greek design where each subsequent rectangle is built on the diagonal of the previous one. The Fibonacci sequence is a more recent discovery, but relies on the same principle of gnomonic growth.

The drawing below shows a cutaway cross section of the Aztec temple of Tenayuca, revealing five gnomic reconstructions, made every 52 years, when their calendar, inherited from the Mayans, was reset and all buildings renewed.

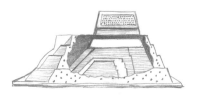

TRIANGULAR *numbers*
Here the sequence 1, 3, 6, 10
increases in a triangular fashion.

RECTANGULAR *numbers*
Here the sequence 2, 6, 12, 20
increases in a musical fashion.

SQUARE *and* **CUBIC** *numbers*
Here the square faces 1, 4, 9, 16
and the cubes 1, 8, 27, 64.

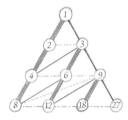

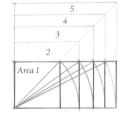

The **LAMBDOMA**
The heavier line shows the octave (2:1), while down
the other side, numbers triple. Also present are the
fifth (3:2), fourth (4:3), and wholetone (9:8).

PROPORTIONAL RECTANGLES
Starting with a square side 1, each successive
rectangle is built on the diagonal of the previous
one to create squares of area 2, 3, 4, and 5.

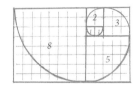

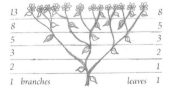

The **GOLDEN SPIRAL.**
Starting with a square we build new squares to create
a spiral of squares, which grows and grows by the magic
Fibonacci sequence 1, 1, 2, 3, 5, 8, 13, 21, 34, 55.

THE NUMBERS OF GROWTH
The Fibonacci sequence appears in many living
things. Here we see it in the number of leaves
and branches of a simple meadow daisy.

TIME AND SPACE
cosmology and manifest number

Looking around us, there are local numbers that particularly manifest around Earth, in our heavens, and in our sciences.

There are, for instance, twelve full moons in a solar year, but the twelfth falls eleven days short of the end, which means that a twelve-moon year, like the Islamic calendar, slides slowly against the solar year, coming round again after 33 years, three elevens.

Other sun-moon marriage numbers are 18 and 19; eclipses repeat after 18 years, and full moon dates repeat after 19 years. Stonehenge displays this as 19 stones in its inner horseshoe. Two full moons occur every 59 days, and Stonehenge records this in its outer circle of 30 stones, one of which is half-width.

Venus draws a five-fold pattern around Earth every eight years allowing us to draw an amazing diagram (*opposite centre*). In those eight years there are almost exactly 99 full moons, nine elevens, the number of divine names in Islam. Jupiter draws an eleven-fold pattern around Earth (*opposite top*).

The numbers of many longer cycles, such as the Great Year, or precession, are also rich in secret qualities. Each great month, such as the Age of Pisces, or Aquarius, lasts 2,160 years, also the diameter of the Moon in miles. Twelve great months give the ancient Western value of 25,920 years for the whole cycle.

The ancient Maya were superb stargazers. Their calendar synchronised not just the Sun and Moon, but also Venus and Mars. They worked out that 81 (or 3 x 3 x 3 x 3) full moons occur exactly every 2392 (or 8 x 13 x 23) days, an astonishingly accurate gearing.

BABYLON, SUMER, AND EGYPT
early number systems

Around 3000 BC the Sumerians developed the earliest writing we know of and with it a base-60 number system (*see page 48*). A particularly useful number, 60 is divisible by 1, 2, 3, 4, 5 and 6.

Working in base-60 gives number patterns different from our modern base-10 system; a Sumerian clay tablet impressed with a cuneiform, "wedge–shaped", stylus shows the 36 times table opposite. Their base-60 system survives today as our measure-ment of cycles and circles with 60 seconds in a minute, 60 minutes in an hour, or degree, and 6 x 60 = 360 degrees in a circle.

Ancient Egyptian numerals were made of characters standing for 1, 10, 100, and so on. An example of Egyptian arithmetic is their method of multiplication, which uses repeated doubling followed by selective addition to find the answer.

The ancient vision of number is a musical one in which every number inverts in the mirror of Unity, two becoming a half, three becoming a third, and so on. In base-60 this reciprocation is especially beautiful, as all multiples of 2, 3, 4, 5, and 6 become simple fractions. For example 15 becomes a quarter. The Babylonians inherited and used this system to invoke their gods.

Egyptian fractions used a mouth heiroglyph (*below*), while fractions of volume were represented using the Eye of Horus.

| ⅕ | ⅟₁₀₀ | ½ | ⅔ | ¾ | ⅟₂₂₉ |

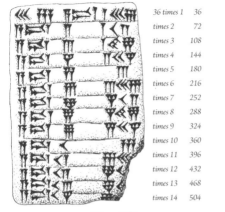

36 times 1	36
times 2	72
times 3	108
times 4	144
times 5	180
times 6	216
times 7	252
times 8	288
times 9	324
times 10	360
times 11	396
times 12	432
times 13	468
times 14	504

36 Times Table

> 1	7
> 2	14
4	28
> 8	56
16	112
> 32	224
(43×7)	301

Egyptian Multiplication

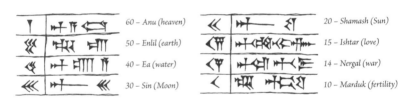

		60 – Anu (heaven)
		50 – Enlil (earth)
		40 – Ea (water)
		30 – Sin (Moon)
		20 – Shamash (Sun)
		15 – Ishtar (love)
		14 – Nergal (war)
		10 – Marduk (fertility)

Numbers of the Gods

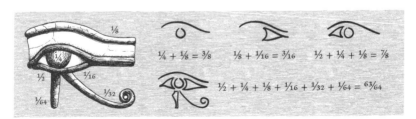

$\frac{1}{4} + \frac{1}{8} = \frac{3}{8}$ $\frac{1}{8} + \frac{1}{16} = \frac{3}{16}$ $\frac{1}{2} + \frac{1}{4} + \frac{1}{8} = \frac{7}{8}$

$\frac{1}{2} + \frac{1}{4} + \frac{1}{8} + \frac{1}{16} + \frac{1}{32} + \frac{1}{64} = \frac{63}{64}$

The Eye of Horus – Fractions of Volume

ANCIENT ASIA
manipulating in tens

In China a written decimal system with 13 basic characters has been used for more than 3,000 years (*see page 48*). Another particularly beautiful system of writing numbers is the *suan zí* or *sangi* rod notation, complete with a small zero, used in China, Japan, and Korea in some form since at least 200 BC (*below*). Later, the famous Chinese abacus replaced rod-numeral counting boards. The speed of its operators, particularly in the Far East, is legendary, and it is still in widespread use today.

India has an ancient numerical tradition. Number is prominent in many of its scriptures, and Indian cosmology uses huge numbers rivaled today only by those of modern physics. Indian numerals originate with the Brahmi sytem of numerals, with 45 characters for the numbers 1 to 90,000. In time the speculations of Indian mathematicians required a new system combining the first nine number names with powers of ten. Rapid and elegant calculation techniques and the unlimited description of very large numbers resulted. The zero also emerged, to denote an empty decimal power without confusion.

It is from India that we received, via the Arabs, our modern decimal place value system.

36

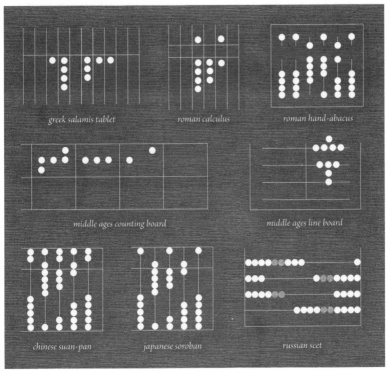

greek salamis tablet

roman calculus

roman hand-abacus

middle ages counting board

middle ages line board

chinese suan-pan

japanese soroban

russian scet

the number 9360 on various counting boards

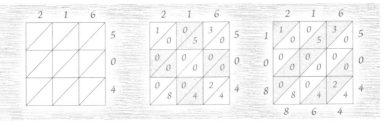

an arabic use of indian numerals - 216 multiplied by 504 equals 108864

GEMATRIA
talking numbers and secret codes

The Phoenicians used a very neat twenty-two-letter consonant alphabet to encode the sounds of their tongue. In time this script was adopted by most Mediterranean peoples and through its Latin variation came to be the alphabet that we use today.

Gematria uses letters as number symbols, so language becomes mathematics. Important canonical, geometrical, musical, metro-logical, and cosmological numbers are defined by many key terms in ancient texts. First appearing widely in ancient Greece, gematria was subsequently adapted to both Hebrew and Arabic where it is known as *abjad*. A simplified system also exists in all three languages using the same values without the zeros.

The example below shows two related phrases connected through an identical sum. It gives some idea of the magical and simultaneous resonance between words and numbers that any literate and numerate reader would have experienced, since for more than 1,000 years gematria was not merely an occult specialty but the standard way of representing numbers.

This secret science is still used today by mystics and sorcerers who use its connections between words, phrases, and number for their mystical significance and talismanic power.

The Holy Spirit				Fountain of Wisdom	
ΤΟ	ΑΓΙΟΝ	ΠΝΕΥΜΑ	= 1080 =	ΠΗΓΗ	ΣΟΦΙΑΣ
300.70	1.3.10.70.50	80.50.5.400.40.1		80.8.3.8	200.70.500.10.1.200
370	134	576		99	981

Archaic Phoenician		Greek			Hebrew		Arabic East | West		Value
'aleph	𐤀	alpha	A	α	aleph	א	'alif	ا	1
bet	𐤁	beta	B	β	bet	ב	ba	ب	2
gimmel	𐤂	gamma	Γ	γ	gimmel	ג	jim	ج	3
dalet	𐤃	delta	Δ	δ	dalet	ד	dal	د	4
he	𐤄	epsilon	E	ε	he	ה	ha	ه	5
waw	𐤅	digamma	F	ς	vov	ו	waw	و	6
zayin	𐤆	zeta	Z	ζ	zayin	ז	za	ز	7
ḥet	𐤇	eta	H	η	het	ח	ḥa	ح	8
ṭet	𐤈	theta	Θ	θ	tet	ט	ṭa	ط	9
yod	𐤉	iota	I	ι	yod	י	ya	ي	10
kaf	𐤊	kappa	K	κ	kof	כ	kaf	ك	20
lamed	𐤋	lambda	Λ	λ	lamed	ל	lam	ل	30
mem	𐤌	mu	M	μ	mem	מ	mim	م	40
nun	𐤍	nu	N	ν	nun	נ	nun	ن	50
samekh	𐤎	ksi	Ξ	ξ	samekh	ס	sin/ṣad	ص س	60
'ayin	𐤏	omicron	O	o	ayin	ע	'ayn	ع	70
pe	𐤐	pi	Π	π	pé	פ	fa	ف	80
ṣade	𐤑	qoppa	Q	ϙ	tsade	צ	ṣad/ḍad	ض ص	90
qof	𐤒	rho	P	ρ	quf	ק	qaf	ق	100
resh	𐤓	sigma	Σ	σ	resh	ר	ra	ر	200
shin	𐤔	tau	T	τ	shin	ש	shin/sin	س ش	300
taw	𐤕	upsilon	Υ	υ	tav	ת	ta	ت	400
		phi	Φ	φ	kof	ך	tha	ث	500
		chi	X	χ	mem	ם	kha	خ	600
		psi	Ψ	ψ	nun	ן	dhal	ذ	700
		omega	Ω	ω	pé	ף	ḍad/ḍha	ظ ض	800
		san	ϡ	ϡ	tsade	ץ	dha/ghayn	غ ظ	900
							ghayn/shin	ش غ	1000

The Greek system includes the disused letters *digamma* and *qoppa* in their original order and reinserts the disused *san* at the end. Likewise the Hebrew system uses five special 'end of word' letter forms to reach 900. In the Arabic system the letters for 60, 90, 300, 800, 900 & 1000 differ in the West and the East of the Islamic world.

MAGIC SQUARES
when it all adds up

Magic squares are a fascinating way of arranging numbers, and there are whole books about them and their secret uses. The magic sum of any square is the same whichever line is added.

Seven magic squares are traditionally associated with the planets (*opposite*). The three-by-three square is Saturn's, and the squares increase by one order as they descend through each planetary sphere to reach the lunar nine-by-nine square. Elegant patterns of odd and even numbers occur in these squares (*shaded in the diagrams*). Each planet also has a magic seal based on the structure of its square, a useful code for wizards.

A magic square is an example of a permutation, ordering things in a set in a particular way. There are eight ways to sum to fifteen using three numbers from one to nine, and all eight ways are present in the three-by-three magic square.

Other totals found in magic squares are worth a second look. The Maya would surely have delighted in the fact that the eight-by-eight square has the magic sum of 13 x 20, while the solar line total of eleventy-one gives an ominous 666 square sum.

With gematria as an additional magical key, words and magic squares naturally interweave in the secret world of spells and other talismanic arts (*see example below*).

square sum = ١+ب+ج+د+ه+و+ز+ح+ط = 45

ادم *Adam* = 1+4+40 = 45 = 7+8+30 = زحل *zuhal (Saturn)*

حواء *Hawwa (Eve)* = 8+6+1 = 15 = *magic sum*

♄

4	9	2
3	5	7
8	1	6

magic sum 15
square sum 45

☽

37	78	29	70	21	62	13	54	5
6	38	79	30	71	22	63	14	46
47	7	39	80	31	72	23	55	15
16	48	8	40	81	32	64	24	56
57	17	49	9	41	73	33	65	25
26	58	18	50	1	42	74	34	66
67	27	59	10	51	2	43	75	35
36	68	19	60	11	52	3	44	76
77	28	69	20	61	12	53	4	45

magic sum 369
square sum 3321

♃

4	14	15	1
9	7	6	12
5	11	10	8
16	2	3	13

magic sum 34
square sum 136

♂

11	24	7	20	3
4	12	25	8	16
17	5	13	21	9
10	18	1	14	22
23	6	19	2	15

magic sum 65
square sum 325

☿

8	58	59	5	4	62	63	1
49	15	14	52	53	11	10	56
41	23	22	44	45	19	18	48
32	34	35	29	28	38	39	25
40	26	27	37	36	30	31	33
17	47	46	20	21	43	42	24
9	55	54	12	13	51	50	16
64	2	3	61	60	6	7	57

magic sum 260
square sum 2080

☉

6	32	3	34	35	1
7	11	27	28	8	30
19	14	16	15	23	24
18	20	22	21	17	13
25	29	10	9	26	12
36	5	33	4	2	31

magic sum 111
square sum 666

♀

22	47	16	41	10	35	4
5	23	48	17	42	11	29
30	6	24	49	18	36	12
13	31	7	25	43	19	37
38	14	32	1	26	44	20
21	39	8	33	2	27	45
46	15	40	9	34	3	28

magic sum 175
square sum 1225

MYTH, GAME, AND RHYME
numbers we grow up with

Some of our earliest experiences with number occur by way of games, rhymes, stories, and cultural myths, many of which are treasure troves of hidden numerical relationships.

Ancient forms of language were regularly number-based, so in poetry we find triplets (three lines of verse), quatrains (verses of four lines), pentameters (lines with five stressed syllables), hexameters (lines with six stressed syllables), and haiku (a three line poem of seventeen syllables, five, seven, then five).

Games, like myths and stories, can store information. The sum of a pack of playing cards, counting jack, queen and king as 11, 12, and 13, is 364, which with the joker produces 365, the number of days in a year. The eighteens and nineteens of the Chinese game of Go echo the cycles of the Sun and the Moon (*see page 32*). These ancient games reflect eternal principles, suggesting larger cosmic games, also with number at their centre.

Almost all games are dependent upon number for both their structure and rules. Imagine a game of tennis played by people who couldn't count higher than three! Below are two examples of knights tours from chess, both of which produce magic squares when numbered in sequence.

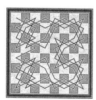
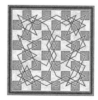

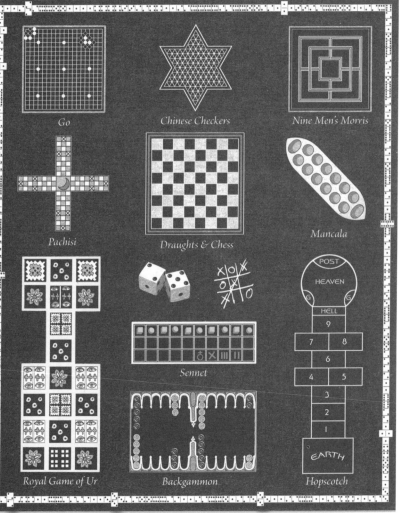

Go

Chinese Checkers

Nine Men's Morris

Pachisi

Draughts & Chess

Mancala

Royal Game of Ur

Sennet

Backgammon

Hopscotch

POST

HEAVEN

G   G

HELL

9

7   8

6

4   5

3

2

1

EARTH

MODERN NUMBERS
the dawn of quantity

When the ancient Greeks proved that the diagonals of squares could not be expressed as fractions, it is said to have caused a crisis in their ranks, a little like the terror still experienced today by many people faced with a square root symbol.

The last 400 years of human thought have transformed our conception of number. After the revolutionary adoption of Indian numerals, and with them the astonishing zero, the next piece of witchcraft was the introduction of negative numbers, thus creating a number line which vanished in two directions.

Negative numbers seem simple enough to us today but they throw up a serious conundrum. Square a negative number and it becomes positive, so what are the square roots of negative numbers? Mathematicians had to invent them! They realized that there was another number line, that of the square roots of negative numbers, which they called *imaginary* numbers, labeled today with an *i* (so *i* is the square root of minus one). The play between imaginary and real numbers effortlessly produces fractals, the recursive shapes we find all around us in nature.

With the decimal system we use today, we can describe numbers like π, or *pi*, the ratio between a circle's circumference and its diameter, with great accuracy. However, some of the most beautiful objects in modern mathematics simply employ repeated fractions which would have been familiar to the ancients. These capture the complex essence of square roots, the golden section (ϕ), π, and the exponential growth function, *e*.

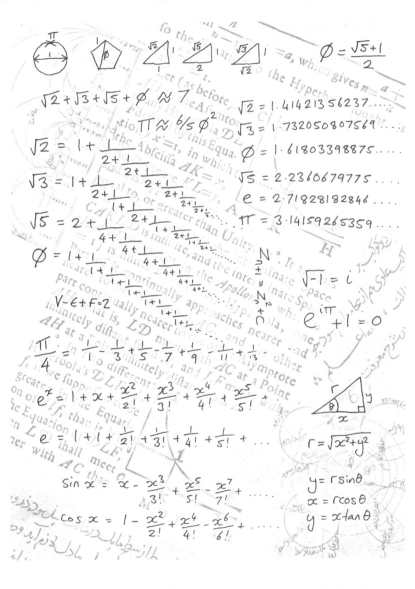

$$\phi = \frac{\sqrt{5}+1}{2}$$

$$\sqrt{2} + \sqrt{3} + \sqrt{5} + \phi \approx 7$$

$$\sqrt{2} = 1.41421356237\ldots$$
$$\sqrt{3} = 1.732050807569\ldots$$

$$\pi \approx 6/5 \, \phi^2$$

$$\phi = 1.61803398875\ldots$$

$$\sqrt{2} = 1 + \cfrac{1}{2 + \cfrac{1}{2 + \cfrac{1}{2 + \cfrac{1}{2 + \cdots}}}}$$

$$\sqrt{3} = 1 + \cfrac{1}{1 + \cfrac{1}{2 + \cfrac{1}{1 + \cfrac{1}{2 + \cdots}}}}$$

$$\sqrt{5} = 2.2360679775\ldots$$
$$e = 2.71828182846\ldots$$
$$\pi = 3.14159265359\ldots$$

$$\sqrt{5} = 2 + \cfrac{1}{4 + \cfrac{1}{4 + \cfrac{1}{4 + \cfrac{1}{4 + \cdots}}}}$$

$$\phi = 1 + \cfrac{1}{1 + \cfrac{1}{1 + \cfrac{1}{1 + \cfrac{1}{1 + \cdots}}}}$$

$$\sqrt{-1} = i$$

$$e^{i\pi} + 1 = 0$$

$$V - \epsilon + F = 2$$

$$\frac{\pi}{4} = \frac{1}{1} - \frac{1}{3} + \frac{1}{5} - \frac{1}{7} + \frac{1}{9} - \frac{1}{11} + \frac{1}{13} - \cdots$$

$$e^x = 1 + x + \frac{x^2}{2!} + \frac{x^3}{3!} + \frac{x^4}{4!} + \frac{x^5}{5!} + \cdots$$

$$e = 1 + 1 + \frac{1}{2!} + \frac{1}{3!} + \frac{1}{4!} + \frac{1}{5!} + \cdots$$

$$r = \sqrt{x^2 + y^2}$$

$$\sin x = x - \frac{x^3}{3!} + \frac{x^5}{5!} - \frac{x^7}{7!} + \cdots$$

$$y = r\sin\theta$$
$$x = r\cos\theta$$
$$y = x\tan\theta$$

$$\cos x = 1 - \frac{x^2}{2!} + \frac{x^4}{4!} - \frac{x^6}{6!} + \cdots$$

ZERO
nothing left to say

Zero has been left until last, because in a sense it is not actually a number at all, just a mark representing the absence of number. It is perhaps for this reason, and the horror many theologians had of it, that nothing took such a long time to emerge as something at all, and in quite a few sensible cultures it never did.

A symbol for zero has been invented independently at least three times. The Babylonians in 400 BC started using the shape of two wedges pressed into clay to act as an "empty place" marker in their sexagesimal numerals, "no number in this column". On the other side of the world, and nearly a thousand years later, the Mayans adopted a seashell symbol for the same function.

The circular form that "nothing" assumed under the Indians reflected the indentation left in sand when a pebble used for counting is removed. Thus our modern zero, inherited from the Indians, began as the visible trace of something no longer there.

Like one, zero probes the borderline between absence and presence. In early Indian mathematical treatises it is referred to as *Sunya*, meaning "void", calling to mind the abyss, the ultimate unknowable, the pregnant ground of all being.

It is perhaps appropriate that our zero takes the form of a circle, itself a symbol of one, and that our one takes the form of a short line between two points. As acknowledged in gematria, each number already contains the seed of its successor within it, and the symbols for zero and one strangely combine to create the golden symbol ϕ, a fitting thought with which to end this book.

EARLY NUMBER SYSTEMS

The ancient systems below all use small sets of characters to represent a limited range of numbers. Those from the ancient Mediterranean repeat marks like a tally stick to make some numbers while the Chinese system combines the characters for one to nine with characters meaning 10, 100, 1,000 and 10,000. In all these systems a number such as 57 would be written as the characters or characters for 50 followed by the character for 7 with no use of place value.

	Egyptian Hieroglyphs	Egyptian Cursive	Cretan 'Linear B'	Greek Attic (Athens)	Sheba (South Arabia)	Early Roman	Medieval Roman	Archaic Chinese	Chinese Seal Script	Classical Chinese
1	ı	ı	ı	Ι	Ι	I	I	一		一
2	ıı	ıı	‖	ΙΙ	ΙΙ	II	II	二		二
3	ııı	ııı	‖ı	ΙΙΙ	ΙΙΙ	III	III	三		三
4	ıııı	ıııı	‖‖	ΙΙΙΙ	ΙΙΙΙ	IIII	IV	亖		四
5			‖‖ı	Γ	Ψ	V	V	乂		五
6			‖‖‖	ΓΙ	ΨΙ	VI	VI	Λ		六
7			‖‖‖ı	ΓΙΙ	ΨΙΙ	VII	VII	+		七
8			‖‖‖‖	ΓΙΙΙ	ΨΙΙΙ	VIII	VIII	)(		八
9			‖‖‖‖ı	ΓΙΙΙΙ	ΨΙΙΙΙ	VIIII	IX			九
10	∩	∧	—	Δ	ο	X	X	—|		十
20	∩∩		=	ΔΔ	οο	XX	XX	=|		二十
30			≡	ΔΔΔ	οοο	XXX	XXX	≡|		三十
40			≡	ΔΔΔΔ	οοοο	XXXX	XL			四十
50			≡		ⴷ	Ψ	L			五十
60			≡≡		ⴷο	ΨX	LX	Λ|		六十
70			≡≡		ⴷοο	ΨXX	LXX	+|		七十
80			≡≡≡		ⴷοοο	ΨXXX	LXXX	)(|		八十
90			≡≡≡		ⴷοοοο	ΨXXXX	XC			九十
100			○	Η			C			一百
500			○○				D			五百
1,000			◇	Χ			M			一千
5,000			○○◇							五千
10,000			◈	Μ						一萬

Place Value Number Systems

Systems of numerals that use position or 'place value' to signify the magnitude of a given digit are few and far between. The earliest such system is Sumerian cuneiform. Stylus impressions in clay are repeated to make glyps for 1 to 59, with place value denoting larger numbers. Later the Babylonians introduced an 'empty place' marker effectively making the first zero.

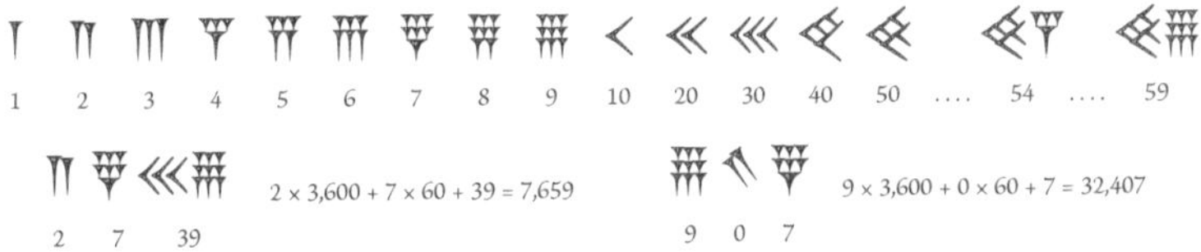
1 2 3 4 5 6 7 8 9 10 20 30 40 50 .... 54 59
2 × 3,600 + 7 × 60 + 39 = 7,659
2 7 39
9 × 3,600 + 0 × 60 + 7 = 32,407
9 0 7

The Maya independently discovered place value and the use of zero. Their base 20 system is usually written vertically. Digits in the 3rd place are not 20 but 18 times those in the second, probably because of the calendrical use of 360.

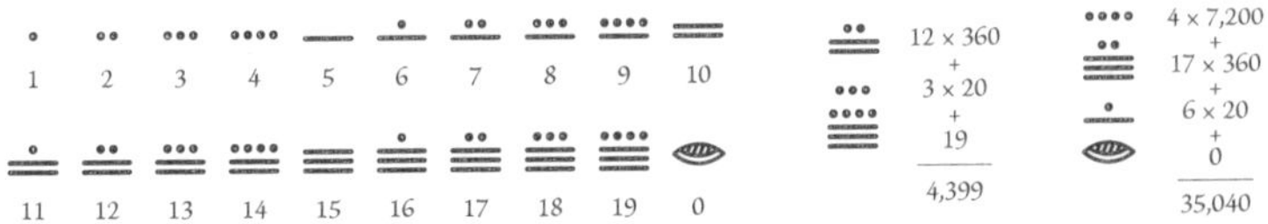
1 2 3 4 5 6 7 8 9 10
11 12 13 14 15 16 17 18 19 0
12 × 360 + 3 × 20 + 19
4,399
4 × 7,200 + 17 × 360 + 6 × 20 + 0
35,040

Far Eastern rod numerals alternate two versions of nine glyphs. The small Indian zero was adopted in the 18th century.

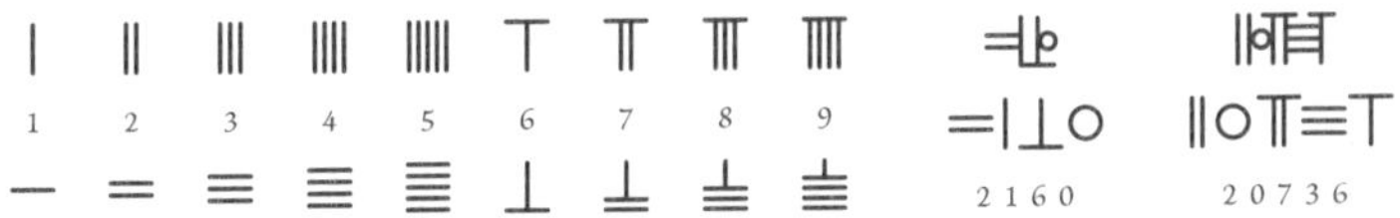
1 2 3 4 5 6 7 8 9
2 1 6 0
2 0 7 3 6

Our own number system originates in Indian Brahmi numerals. From the 6th century onwards variations of the first 9 Brahmi digits were used with a small circular zero in a place value system. This system was passed to Europe by the Arabs.

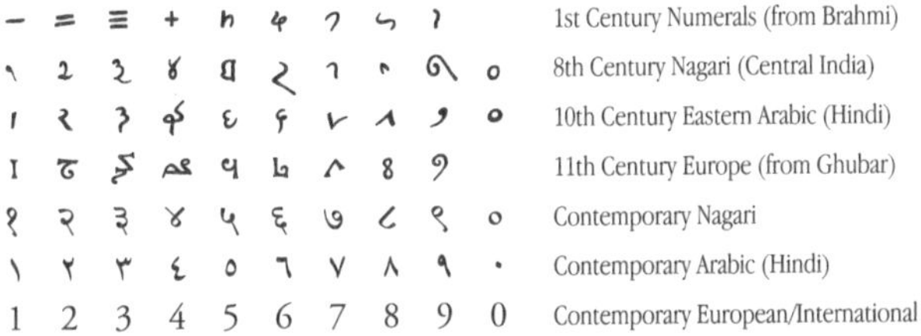
1st Century Numerals (from Brahmi)
8th Century Nagari (Central India)
10th Century Eastern Arabic (Hindi)
11th Century Europe (from Ghubar)
Contemporary Nagari
Contemporary Arabic (Hindi)
1 2 3 4 5 6 7 8 9 0
Contemporary European/International

PYTHAGOREAN NUMBERS

Triangular Numbers
sum of numbers
1 + 2 + 3 + 4 ...
1, 3, 6, 10, 15 ...

Centered Triangular Nums
triangles increase by 3
1 + 3 + 6 + 9 ...
1, 4, 10, 19 ...

Tetrahedral Numbers
sum of triangular nums.
1 + 3 + 6 + 10 ...
1, 4, 10, 20 ...

Rectangular Numbers
twice triangular nums.
also 2 + 4 + 6 + 8 ...
2, 6, 12, 20 ...

Square Numbers
sum of odd numbers
1 + 3 + 5 + 7 + 9 + ...
1, 4, 9, 16, 25 ...

Centered Square Nums
squares increase by 4
1 + 4 + 8 + 12 + ...
1, 5, 13, 25 ...

Cubic Numbers
1x1x1, 2x2x2,
3x3x3, 4x4x4 ...
1, 8, 27, 64 ...

Square Numbers
as sum of two adjacent
triangular numbers.
here 10 + 15 = 25

Pentagonal Numbers
split into threes
1 + 4 + 7 + 10 + 13 + ...
1, 5, 12, 22, 35, ...

Centerd Pentagonal Nums
up five more
1 + 5 + 10 + 15 + ...
1, 6, 16, 31, 61 ...

Square Pyramidal Nums
square by square
1 + 4 + 9 + 16 + ...
1, 5, 14, 30, 55 ...

Centered Hexagonal Nums
center and six triangles
1 + 6 + 12 + 18 + ...
1, 7, 19, 37, 61 ...

The 3-4-5 Triangle
area 6, perimeter 12
enclosed circle diameter 2

The 5-12-13 Triangle
area 30, perimeter 30
enclosed circle diameter 4

The 8-15-17 Triangle
area 60, perimeter 40
enclosed circle diameter 6

The 7-24-25 Triangle
area 84, perimeter 56
enclosed circle diameter 6

EXAMPLES OF GEMATRIA

Ancient Greek and Christian gematria;

$$ΙΗΣΟΥΣ + ΧΡΙΣΤΟΣ = 2368$$
(Jesus) 888   (Christ) 1480

$$888 : 1480 : 2368 = 3 : 5 : 8$$

$$ΚΑΙ Ο ΑΡΙΘΜΟΣ ΑΥΤΟΥ ΧΞϚ = 2368$$
(And his number is 666)

$$ΤΟ ΑΓΙΟΝ ΠΝΕΥΜΑ + ΠΑΡΑ ΘΕΟΥ = 1746$$
(The Holy Spirit) 1080   (from God) 666

$$Η ΔΟΞΑ ΤΟΥ ΘΕΟΥ ΙΣΡΑΗΛ = 1746$$
(Glory of The God of Israel)

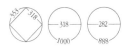

ΕΡΜΗΣ   is to   ΖΕΥΣ
(Hermes) 353   (Zeus) 612

as   ΖΕΥΣ   is to   ΑΠΟΛΛΩΝ
(Zeus) 612   (Apollo) 1061

as   ΚΑΡΠΟΣ   is to   ΖΩΗ
(Fruit) 471   (Life) 815

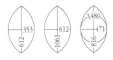

ΗΛΙΟΣ (Sun) = 318   ΒΙΟΣ (Life) = 282

1000 as magnified Unity

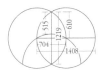

ΠΑΡΘΕΝΟΣ (Virgin) = 515

ΞΥΛΟΝ (Cross) = 610

Ο ΘΕΟΣ ΙΣΡΑΗΛ
(The God of Israel) = 703

ΙΧΘΟΣ (Fish) = 1219

ΣΩΤΗΡ (Saviour) = 1408

The Divine Name YHWH as Tetractys;

י   = 10
ה   י   = 10 + 5 = 15
ו   ה   י   = 10 + 5 + 6 = 21
ה   ו   ה   י   = 10 + 5 + 6 + 5 = 26

היה   HaYaH (He Was) = 25
הוה   HoWeH (He is) = 16
יהיה   YiHYeH (He shall be) = 30

Some Hebrew correspondences;

אהבה   אחד
     = 13 =
AHAVAH (Love)   EKHAD (One)

and their sum = 26 = YHWH

יהוה   חוה   אדם
= 26 =
YHWH   ADAM – KHAWAH

סוד   ייי
= 70 =
SOD (secret)   YAYIN (wine)

or *in vino veritas!*

Hebrew letter names and their totals;

אלף	111 ALEPH		למד	74 LAMED
בית	412 BET		מים	90 MEM
גמל	73 GIMMEL		נון	110 NUN
דלת	434 DALET		סמך	120 SAMEKH
הא	6 HE		עין	130 AYIN
וו	12 VOV		פה	85 PE
זין	67 ZAYIN		צדי	104 TSADE
חית	418 HET		קוף	104 QUF
טית	419 TET		ריש	510 RESH
יוד	20 YOD		שין	360 SHIN
כף	100 KOF		תו	406 TAV

*Every number contains the seed of the
next so the rules of gematria allow a
difference of 1 in comparisons.
Fractional parts in geometric measures
and ratios can be rounded either way.*

Talisman with magic sum of 66, the abjad total for the Divine Name Allah;

21	26	19
20	22	24
25	18	23

Some names of God in abjad order;

الله	66	ALLAH
باقي	113	BAQI (Everlasting)
جامع	114	JAMI (Gatherer)
ديان	65	DAYAN (Judge)
هادي	20	HADI (Guide)
ولي	46	WALI (Friend)
زكي	37	ZAKI (Purifier)
حق	108	HAQ (Truth)
طاهر	215	TAHIR (Pure)
يسين	130	YASSIN (Chief)
كافي	111	KAFI (Sufficient)
لطيف	129	LATIF (Subtle)
ملك	90	MALIK (King)
نور	256	NUR (Light)
سميع	180	SAMI (All Hearing)
علي	110	'ALI (Most High)
فتاح	489	FATAH (Revealer)
صمد	134	SAMAD (Eternal)
قادر	305	QADIR (Powerful)
رب	202	RAB (Lord)
شفيع	460	SHAFI (Healer)
توب	408	TAWAB (Oft Forgiving)
ثابت	903	THABIT (Stable)
خالق	731	KHALIQ (Creator)
ذاكر	921	DHAKIR (Rememberer)
ضار	1,001	DAR (Chastiser)
ظاهر	1,106	DHAHIR (Apparent)
غفور	1,285	GHAFUR (Forgiving)

FURTHER MAGIC SQUARES

A magic square is *normal* if it uses whole numbers from 1 to the square of its order, and *simple* if its only property is rows, columns and main diagonals adding to the magic sum. The normal magic square of order-3 is unique apart from 8 possible reflections and rotations or *aspects* (4 below).

2	7	6
9	5	1
4	3	8

6	7	2
1	5	9
8	3	4

2	9	4
7	5	3
6	1	8

4	9	2
3	5	7
8	1	6

If the numbers in a magic square sum symmetrically about the centre, e.g. 2+8, 7+3... the square is *associated* (not simple), the number pairs are *complementary*.

There are 880 order-4 normal magic squares. To count magic squares mathematicians rotate/reflect them so the top-left cell is as small as possible with the cell to its right less than the cell below. Complementary numbers in normal order-4 squares form 12 *Dudeney patterns* (4 shown below).

2	11	14	7
13	8	1	12
3	10	15	6
16	5	4	9

group I

1	4	15	14
13	16	3	2
8	5	10	11
12	9	6	7

group II

4	14	5	11
15	1	10	8
9	7	16	2
6	12	3	13

group III

1	10	8	15
16	7	9	2
11	4	14	5
6	13	3	12

group IV

The 48 Group I squares are *pandiagonal*, the 6 broken diagonals formed by opposite sides wrapping round to meet each other also sum magically (*below left and centre*).

Order-4 pandiagonal magic squares are also *most-perfect*, any

2-by-2 square, including wrap arounds, adds to the magic sum (*above right*). Only normal pandiagonal squares of doubly-even order (4, 8, 12…) can be most-perfect.

1	15	24	8	17
23	7	16	5	14
20	4	13	22	6
12	21	10	19	3
9	18	2	11	25

There are 275,305,224 normal order-5 magic squares. Order-5 is the lowest order of magic squares that can be both pandiagonal and associated (*one shown here*). There are 36 essentially different pandiagonal order-5 magic squares, each produces 99 variations by permuting rows, columns and diagonals for a total of 3,600 pandiagonal order-5 squares. It is not known how many normal order-6 magic squares there are. Order-6 is the first oddly-even order, divisible by 2 but not by 4, the hardest squares to construct. It is impossible for a normal order-6 square to be pandiagonal or associated.

To construct a magic square of doubly-even order, place the numbers in sequence from top left as below. Using the pattern shown exchange every number on a marked diagonal with its complement and you have a magic square.

To make a magic square of any odd order place 1 in the top middle cell and place numbers in sequence up and to the right by one cell, wrapping top/bottom and right/left as necessary. When a previously filled cell is reached move down one cell instead. The central cell will contain the middle number of the sequence and the diagonals will add to the magic sum (*alternative fill pattern below right*).

Two magic squares combine to make a *composition magic* square with the original orders multiplied together.

1	14	7	12
15	4	9	6
10	5	16	3
8	11	2	13

2	7	6
9	5	1
4	3	8

16	96	80
128	64	0
48	32	112

Make copies of the first square (*left*) as if each were a cell in the second square (*centre*). Subtract 1 from each cell in the second square and multiply by the number of cells in the first square (*right*). Add these to each cell in the large square.

17	30	23	28	97	110	103	108	81	94	87	92
31	20	25	22	111	100	105	102	95	84	89	86
26	21	32	19	106	101	112	99	90	85	96	83
24	27	18	29	104	107	98	109	88	91	82	93
129	142	135	140	65	78	71	76	1	14	7	12
143	132	137	134	79	68	73	70	15	4	9	6
138	133	144	131	74	69	80	67	10	5	16	3
136	139	130	141	72	75	66	77	8	11	2	13
49	62	55	60	33	46	39	44	113	126	119	124
63	52	57	54	47	36	41	38	127	116	121	118
58	53	64	51	42	37	48	35	122	117	128	115
56	59	50	61	40	43	34	45	120	113	114	125

To make a *bordered* magic square add double the order, plus 2 to the cells of a normal magic square and make a border of the highest/lowest numbers in the new sequence.

5	4	24	25	7
3	12	17	10	23
18	11	13	15	8
20	16	9	14	6
19	22	2	1	21

14	10	17	6	18
2	11	25	5	24
19	5	13	21	7
22	23	1	15	4
8	16	9	20	12

2	10	19	14	20
22	3	21	11	8
17	25	13	1	9
18	15	5	23	4
6	12	7	16	24

bordered square *inlaid square* *inlaid diamond*

A magic square within another that doesn't follow the highest/lowest number border rule is an *inlaid* magic square. Also possible are *inlaid magic diamonds* and *embedded* magic squares (*orders 3 & 4 in order-7 below*).

9	1	37	48	38	26	16
49	10	23	47	4	18	24
15	22	36	11	29	42	20
7	33	44	25	43	17	6
35	46	14	2	21	27	30
19	32	8	3	28	40	45
41	31	13	39	12	5	34

A *bimagic* square is still magic if all its numbers are squared. This one has a magic sum of 369. Each 3-by-3 section also has this sum. The 'squared' magic sum is 20,049.

1	23	18	33	52	38	62	75	67
48	40	35	77	72	55	25	11	6
65	60	79	13	8	21	45	28	50
43	29	51	66	58	80	14	9	19
63	73	68	2	24	16	31	53	39
26	12	4	46	41	36	78	70	56
76	71	57	27	10	5	47	42	34
15	7	20	44	30	49	64	59	81
32	54	37	61	74	69	3	22	17

In 3 dimensions we find the surprising possibility of magic cubes. There are 4 order-3 normal magic cubes (*2 shown below*) each has 48 aspects. All rows, columns, pillars and the four long diagonals from opposite vertices sum to 42.

Even more remarkably magic figures in 4-dimensions, once considered impossible, were first discovered by John R. Hendricks who sketched a magic tesseract, or 4-D cube, in 1950. Below is one of 58 normal order-3 magic tesseracts.

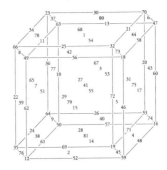

SOME NUMBERS OF THINGS

1

One One (UNIVERSAL).

2

Two Forces (TAOIST): Receptive (yin), Active (yang).
Two Perspectives (UNIVERSAL): Subject, Object.
Two Polarities (GEOGRAPHY): North, South.
Two Polarities (PHYSICS): Positive, Negative.
Two Principles (METAPHYSICS): Essence, Substance.
Two Regents (ALCHEMY): Queen, King.
Two Sides Left, Right.
Two Tribal Types (ANTHROPOLOGY): Settler, Nomad.
Two Truths (LOGIC): Analytic (a priori), Synthetic (a posteriori).
Two Ways of Knowing (RELIGION): Esoteric, Exoteric.

3

The Great Triad (TAOIST): Heaven, Man, Earth.
The Holy Trinity (CHRISTIAN): Father, Son, Holy Ghost.
Three Alchemical Stages (ALCHEMY): Blackening (nigredo), Whitening (albedo), Reddening (rubedo).
Three Aspects of Knowledge (GREEK): The Knower, Knowing, The Known.
Three Dialectic Phases (WESTERN): Thesis, Antithesis, Synthesis.
Three Dimensions (PHYSICAL): Medial, Lateral, Vertical.
Three Fates (GREEK): Spinner (Clotho), Measurer (Lachesis), Cutter (Atropos).
Three Furies (GREEK): Avenging Murder (Tisiphone), Jealousy (Megaera), Unceasing Anger (Alecto).
Three Generation of Quarks (PHYSICS): Up & Down, Charm & strange, Top & Bottom.
Three Graces (GREEK): Splendour (Aglaia), Mirth (Euphrosyne), Good Cheer (Thalia).
Three Gunas (HINDU): Fire (red), Water (white), Earth (black).
Three Kingdoms (MEDIEVAL): Animal, Vegetable, Mineral.
Three Modes (ASTROLOGY): Cardinal, Fixed, Mutable.
Three Parts of the Atom (20TH C): Proton, Neutron, Electron.
Three Parts of a Syllogism (ARISTOTLE): Premise, Universal Principle, Conclusion.
Three Primary Colors (LIGHT): Red, Green, Blue.
Three Principles (ALCHEMY): Sulfur, Mercury, Salt.
Three Qualities (CHRISTIAN): Faith, Hope, Love.
Three Regular Things (GEOMETRY): Triangles, Squares, Hexagons.
Three Revolutionary Virtues (FRENCH): Liberty, Equality, Fraternity.

Three Stages (HINDU): Creating (Brahma), Sustaining (Vishnu), Destroying (Shiva).
Three Stages of the Soul (JAIN): External, Internal, Supreme.
The Trivium (MEDIEVAL): Logic, Rhetoric, Grammar.

4

Four Beautiful Harmonies (MUSIC): Unsion, Octave, Fifth, Fourth. All arise from ratios involving the first four numbers.
Four Castes (HINDU): Holy (Brahmin), Heroic (Kshatriya), Business (Vaisya), Servant (Shudra).
Four Causes (ARISTOTLE): Formal, Material, Efficient, Final.
Four Directions (COMMON): North, South, East, West.
Four Elements (WESTERN): Fire, Earth, Air, Water.
Four Forces (MODERN): Electromagnetic, Strong Nuclear, Weak Nuclear, Gravitational.
Four Humours (WESTERN): Sanguine, Choleric, Phlegmatic, Melancholic.
Four Levels of Psyche (JUNG): Ego, Shadow, Anima/Animus, Self.
Four Modes of Pysche (JUNG): Feeling, Thinking, Sensing, Intuiting.
Four Noble Truths (BUDDHISM): The Truth, Cause, Cessation and Path to cessation of suffering.
Four Seasons (WESTERN): Spring, Summer, Autumn, Winter.
Four Types of Literature (WESTERN): Romance, Tragedy, Irony, Comedy.
The Quadrivium (WESTERN): Number, Music, Geometry, Cosmology.

5

Five Animals (CHINESE): Scaled, Winged, Naked, Furred, Shelled.
Five Directions and Colors (CHINESE): East (green) , South (red), Centre (yellow), West (white), North (black).
Five Elements (CHINESE): Fire, Earth, Metal, Water, Wood.
Five Elements (BUDDHIST): Void, Water, Earth, Fire, Air.
Five Notes (CHINESE): Black keys on a piano.
Five Orders of Architecture (WESTERN): Tuscan, Doric, Ionic, Corinthian, Composite.
Five Parts of the Personality (EGYPTIAN): Name, Shade, Life force (Ka), Character (Ba), Spirit (Akh=Ka+Ba).
Five Platonic Solids (UNIVERSAL): Tetrahedron, Octahedron, Cube, Icosahedron, Dodecahedron.
Five Poisons (BUDDHIST): Confusion, Pride, Envy, Hatred, Desire.
Five Precepts (BUDDHIST): Respect for Life, Respect for Property, Chastity, Sobriety, Speaking the Truth.

Five Senses (COMMON): Sight, Hearing, Touch, Smell, Taste.

Five Sounds (CHINESE): Calling, Laughing, Singing, Lamenting, Moaning.

Five Smells (CHINESE): Goatish, Burning, Fragrant, Rank, Rotten.

Five Tastes (CHINESE): Sour, Bitter, Sweet, Spicy, Salty.

Five Virtues (BUDDHIST): Kindness, Goodness, Respect, Economy, Altruism.

Five Virtues (CHINESE): Benevolence, Propriety, Good Faith, Righteousness, Knowledge.

6

Six Days of Creation (ABRAHAMIC): Light, Firmament, Land & Vegetation, Heavenly Bodies, Fish & Birds, Animals & Man.

Six Directions (COMMON): Up, Down, Left, Right, Front, Back.

Six Kingdoms (MODERN): Archaebacteria & Bacteria (pro-karyotes). Protista, Fungi, Plantae & Animalia (eukaryotes).

Six Perfections (BUDDHISM): Giving, Morality, Patience, Energy, Meditation, Wisdom.

Six Reactions (CHEMISTRY): Synthesis & Decomposition, Combustion, Single & Double Displacement, Acid-Base.

Six Realms (HINDU & BUDDHIST): Gods, Hells, Human, Hungry Ghosts, Demons, Animals.

Six Regular Polytopes (4-DIMENSIONAL SOLIDS): Simplex, Tesseract, 16-Cell, 24-Cell, 120 Cell, 600-cell.

7

Seven Border Geometries (UNIVERSAL): There are seven possible kinds of border symmetry.

Seven Chakras (HINDU): Root (4 petals), Sacral (6), Solar Plexus (10), Heart (12), Throat (16), Brow (2), Crown (1000).

Seven Deadly Sins and their Seven Contrary Virtues (CHRISTIAN): Humility against pride, Kindness against envy, Abstinence against gluttony, Chastity against lust, Patience against anger, Liberality against envy, Diligence against sloth.

Seven Endocrine Glands (MEDICAL): Pineal, Pituitary, Thyroid, Thymus, Adrenal, Pancreas, Gonads.

Seven Heavenly Bodies and their Days (ANCIENT): Moon (Mon), Mercury (Wed), Venus (Fri), Sun (Sun), Mars (Tues), Jupiter (Thurs), Saturn (Sat).

Seven Liberal Arts (WESTERN): Logic, Rhetoric and Grammar (*Trivium*): Number, Music, Geometry, Cosmology (*Quadrivium*).

Seven Metals (ANCIENT): Silver, Mercury, Copper, Gold, Iron, Tin, Lead.

Seven Modes (GREEK): Ionian, Dorian, Phrygian, Lydian, Myxolydian, Aeolian, Locrian: using just the white keys on a piano, these refer to the seven-note scale starting with C, D, E, F, G, A and B, respectively.

Seven Stages of the Soul (SUFI): Compulsion, Conscience, Inspiration, Tranquility, Submission, Servant, Perfected.

Seven Virtues (CHRISTIAN): Faith, Hope, Charity, Fortitude, Justice, Prudence, Temperance.

8

Eight Semi-Regular Tilings (GEOMETRY): There are eight semi-regular tilings in the plane.

Eight Immortals (TAOIST): Youth, Old Age, Poverty, Wealth, The Populace, Nobility, The Masculine, The Feminine.

Eight Limbs of Yoga (VEDIC): Morality (Yama), Observances (Niyama), Postures (Asanas), Breathing (Pranayama), Concentration (Dharana), Devotion (Dhyana), Union (Samadhi).

Eight Trigrams (I-CHING): *Chi'en* (Heaven, Creative), *Tui* (Attraction, achievement), *Li* (Awareness, beauty), *Chen* (Action, movement), *Sun* (Following, Penetration), *K'an* (Danger, Peril), *Ken* (Stop, Rest), *K'un* (Earth, Receptive).

Eightfold Path (BUDDIST): Right View, Right Speech, Right Action, Right Livelihood, Right Effort, Right Mindfulness, Right Concentration.

9

Nine Muses (GREEK): History (Clio), Astronomy (Urania), Tragedy (Melpomene), Comedy (Thalia), Dance (Terpsichore), Songs to the Gods (Polyhymnia), Epic Poetry (Calliope), Love Poetry (Erato), Lyric Poetry (Euterpe).

Nine Orders of Angels (WESTERN): Angels, Archangels, Virtues, Powers, Principalities, Dominations, Throne, Cherubim, Seraphim.

Nine Personalities (MIDDLE-EASTERN): Perfectionist, Giver, Achiever, Tragic Romantic, Observer, Contradictor, Enthusiast, Leader, Mediator.

Nine Regular Polyhedra (UNIVERSAL): The *five Platonic Solids* plus the four stellated polyhedra the great, the stellated, and the great stellated dodecahedra, and the great icosacahedron.

Nine Semi-Regular Tilings (UNIVERSAL): Although there are eight standard patterns, one of these has different left- and right-handed versions, making nine in all.

10

Ten Commandments (CHRISTIANITY): Honour Mother, Father & Sabbath. No other gods, Graven images, Blaspheming, Killing, Adultery, Stealing, False witness, Coveting.

Ten Levels (BUDDHISM): Joyous, Stainless, Light-maker, Radiant, Resilient, Turning toward, Far-going, Unshakeable, Good Mind, Cloud of Dharma.

Ten Sephiroth (KABBALAH): Kether, Chokmah, Binah, Chesed, Geburah, Tiphareth, Netzach, Hod, Yesod, Malkuth.

Select Glossary of Number

1 The 1st triangular, square, pentagonal, hexagonal, tetrahedral, octahedral, cubic, Fibonacci, Lucas num.

2 The 1st even (female) num. The planet Mercury's day is exactly two of its years. Uranus orbital radius is two of Saturns. Neptune's period is twice Uranus'.

3 The 1st Greek odd (masculine) num. $1 + 2$. There are three regular tilings of the plane. After three years the moon closely repeats its phases in the calendar. In engineering triangulation creates stability.

4 The 2nd square num. $2^2 = 2 \times 2 = 2 + 2$. Num of vertices and faces of a tetrahedron. Every integer is the sum of at most 4 squares.

5 Sum of the 1st male and female nums. $1^2 + 2^2$. Five notes in the pentatonic scale. Five Platonic solids. The 5th Fibonacci num and the 2nd pentagonal num.

6 The 3rd triangular num as $6 = 1 + 2 + 3$. The factorial of 3, written $3! = 1 \times 2 \times 3$. Area and semi-perimeter of the 3-4-5 triangle. The f1st perfect num (sum of its factors). Edges on a tetrahedron, faces on a cube, vertices of an octahedron. Six regular 4-D polytopes.

7 There are seven frieze symmetries. Seven notes in the traditional scale. Seven endocrine glands in humans. Sum of spots on opposite sides of a dice. Seven tetrominos (Tetris). 4th Lucas num.

8 The 2nd cube, $2^3 = 2 \times 2 \times 2 = 8$. Faces on an octahedron, vertices on a cube. The 6th Fibonacci num. Eight semi-regular tilings. Bits in a Byte.

9 The square of three. $3^2 = 3 \times 3 = 1^3 + 2^3$. There are nine regular polyhedra and nine semi-regular tilings of the plane if you include the chiral pair. In base 10, the digits of all multiples of 9 eventually sum to 9.

10 The 4th triangular and 3rd tetrahedral num. $= 1^2 + 3^2$.

11 11 dimensions unify the four forces of physics. The 5th Lucas num. Sunspot cycle in years.

12 12 notes complete the equal-tempered scale. The 3rd pentagonal num. 12 spheres touch a central one as the cubeoctahedron. Num of vertices of an icosahedron, faces of a dodecahedron, edges of both cube and octahedron. Petals of the heart chakra.

13 The 7th Fibonacci num. There are 13 Archimedean polyhedra. Appears as the octave (13th note), and in the 5-12-13 triangle. Locusts swarm every 13 years.

14 The 3rd square pyramidal num $= 1^2 + 2^2 + 3^2$. Num of lines in a sonnet (octave, quartet, couplet).

15 Triangular num. Sum in lines of a 3×3 magic square. Balls in a snooker triangle.

16 2^4 and 4^2. Perimeter and area of a 4×4 square. Petals of the throat chakra.

17 The number of 2-D symmetry groups. $1^4 + 2^4$. Syllables in Japanese Haiku $(5 + 7 + 5)$. Tones in Arabic tuning.

18 The number of years in a Saros eclipse cycle before you get a eclipse of the same kind near the same place.

19 The number of years in the Metonic cycle. After 19 years full moons recur on the same calendar dates.

20 The sum of the first 4 triangular numbers. Num of faces in an icosahedron, vertices in a dodecahedron. Days in a Mayan month. Amino acids in humans.

21 The 6th triangular and 8th Fibonacci num. 3×7. Letters in the Italian alphabet.

22 Max. num of pieces into which a cake can be cut with 6 slices. Channels in the Kabbala. Letters in the Hebrew alphabet. Major Arcana in Tarot. Tones in Indian tuning.

23 Chromosome pairs make a human.

24 Spheres can touch one in 4-D. Letters in Greek alphabet. $4! = 1 \times 2 \times 3 \times 4$.

25 $5^2 = 3^2 + 4^2$.

26 The only number to sit between a square and a cube. Num of letters in Latin and English alphabets.

27 $3^3 = 3 \times 3 \times 3$. The number of nakshatras into which the ecliptic is divided in Hindu cosmology.

28 The 2nd perfect num, sum of its factors. Triangular. Num of letters in Arabic and Spanish alphabets.

29 A Lucas num, the series goes 1, 3, 4, 7, 11, 18, 29 etc. Letters in Norwegian alphabet.

30 Edges on both dodecahedra and icosahedra. Area and perimeter of a Pythagorean 5-12-13 triangle. The Moon orbits the Earth at a distance of 30 Earth diameters.

31 Planes of existence in Buddhism. A Mersenne prime, of the form $2^n - 1$, where n is prime.

32 2^5. The smallest 5th power besides 1. Num of crystal classes. Num of Earth diameters to reach the Moon.

33 $1! + 2! + 3! + 4!$. Num of vertebrae in the human spinal column, carrying 33 pairs of nerves. There are 12053 sunrises in 33 years.

34 The sum in the lines of a 4×4 magic square.

35 Sum of Pythagorean harmonic sequence 12:9:8:6. Also the sum of the first five triangular numbers.

36 $1^3 + 2^3 + 3^3$. 8th triangular and 6th square num.

37 The root of the 111, 222 ... 666, 777, 888 sequence. 37 moons in 3 years. Stages of the Buddhist bodhisattva.

40 The number of fingers and toes of a man and woman together. 40 Spheres can touch one in 5 dimensions.

42 The sum in the lines of a 3-D $3 \times 3 \times 3$ magic square.

50 Num of letters in sanscrit alphabet, petals of all chakras excluding crown.

52 Num of playing cars in a pack, teeth a human gets in a life. The Mayan calendar round was 52 years, at which point the 260 day Tzolkin and the 365 day Haab reset.

55 Highest triangular & Fibonacci num (others 1, 3, 21).

56 Station stones at Stonehenge. Useful for eclipse prediction. 7×8. The product of $1 + 2 + 4$ and $1 \times 1 \times 2 \times 4$. Tetrahedral. Minor Arcana in Tarot.

59 There are two full moons every 59 days. Prime.

60 $3 \times 4 \times 5$. Basis of Sumerian and Babylonian counting. Smallest number divisible by 1 through 6.

61 Codons specify amino acids in human mRNA.

64 Eight squared, four cubed and 2^6. Num of hexagrams in the I-Ching, squares on a chess-board. 64 codons specify amino acids in human DNA.

65 The sum in the lines of a 5×5 magic square.

71 The Hindu Indra lives for 71 eons.

72 Spheres can touch one in 6 dimensions. 360/5. 72 names of God in Kabbala. 1 lifetime = 1 precessional 'Great Day' or 360th of a Great Year = 72 years.

73 73 Tzolkin = 52 Haab in the Mayan calendar.

76 Years between sightings of Halley's comet.

78 Complete Tarot, 22 major and 56 minor Arcana.

81 The square of nine. 3^4. There are 81 stable elements.

56

91	A quarter of a year, 7 x 13.
92	Elements can occur in nature; all others appear fleetingly under laboratory conditions.
99	Names of Allah. 99 full moons occur in 8 years.
100	= 10 x 10 in any base.
108	1^1 x 2^2 x 3^3. The Sun diameter is 109 times Earth's, and its distance from Earth is 107 Sun diams. Num of Hindu and Buddhist prayer beads.
111	The sum in the lines of a 6 x 6 magic square. Num of Moon diameters between Moon and Earth.
120	1 x 2 x 3 x 4 x 5. Triangular and tetrahedral.
121	The square of eleven.
125	The cube of five.
128	2^7. The largest num not the sum of distinct squares.
144	The square of 12. Only square Fibonacci num.
153	The number of fishes in the net in St. John's Gospel, XX1.11. = 1^3 + 3^3 + 5^3 = 1! + 2! + 3! + 4! + 5! = the square of the number of full moons in a year. Archimedes' approximation for √3 was 265/153
169	The square of thirteen.
175	The sum in the lines of a 7 x 7 magic square.
206	Bones in an adult human body.
216	Plato's nuptial number. The smallest cube that is the sum of three cubes, 6^3 = 3^3 + 4^3 + 5^3. Twice 108.
219	There are 219 3-D symmetry groups.
220	Member of the smallest amicable pair with 284, the factors of each summing to the other.
235	The number of full moons in a 19-year Metonic cycle.
243	3^5. Appears in the leimma, the Pythagorean halftone 256:243 between the third and fourth notes.
256	2^8. In computers, the maximum value of a byte.
260	The Mayan Tzolkin, 20 x 13 = 260 days. Magic sum of 8 x 8 magic square.
284	Amicable with 220, summing with it to 504.
300	Babies are born with 300 bones..
343	The cube of 7.
354	Days in 12 full moons, or the Islamic year.
360	3 x 4 x 5 x 6. Degrees in a circle. Days in a Mayan Tun.
361	The square of 19. A Chinese Go board is 19 by 19.
364	The number of pips on a pack of playing cards, counting J=11, Q=12, K=13. Also = 4 x 7 x 13.
365	The Mayan Haab, consisted of 18 months of 20 days each, plus five days added on (Wayeb) to make 365.
369	Magic sum of 9 x 9 magic square.
384	Root number for Pythagorean musical scale.
400	The Sun is 400 times larger than the Moon, and 400 times further away.
432	72 x 6. 108 x 4. Second note in Pythagorean scale, 9/8 up from 384.
486	Pythagorean major third, two tones up from 384.
496	The third perfect num, sum of its factors.
504	7 x 8 x 9.
512	2^9. Fourth, 4:3 (or 9/8 x 9/8 x 256/243) up from 384. The cube of 8.
540	There are 540 double doors to Valhalla. Half 1080.
576	Perfect fifth, 3:2 up from 384. 24^2.
584	Venus' synodic period in days. = 8 x 73.
648	Pythagorean sixth, 3:2 up from the second (432).
666	Sum of numbers 1 to 36. Yang principle in gematria. The sum of the first six Roman numerals (I V X L C D).
720	6! = 1 x 2 x 3 x 4 x 5 x 6 = 8 x 9 x 10. 2 x 360.
729	Pythagorean seventh, 3:2 up from the third (486). The cube of 9. 3^6 or 27^2. Appears in Plato's *Republic*.
780	Mars' synodic period, in days. = 13 x 60.
873	1! + 2! + 3! + 4! + 5! + 6!.
880	Num of substantially different 4 x 4 magic squares.
1000	The cube of 10 in any base.
1080	2^3 x 3^3 x 5. Canonical. Yin principle in gematria. Radius of Moon in miles.
1225	The second triangular and square num. 35^2.
1331	The cube of 11.
1461	There are 1461 days in 4 years.
1540	One of only five triangular AND tetrahedral nums.
1728	The cube of 12. Cubic inches in a cubic foot.
1746	Canonical. The sum of 666 and 1080.
2160	720 x 3. Canonical. Diameter of Moon in miles. Years in a precessional "great month" or astrological age.
2178	3^7.
2392	= 8 x 13 x 23. The Maya discovered that 3^4 = 81 full moons occur every 2392 days to astonishing accuracy.
2920	= 584 x 5 = 365 x 8. The number of days it takes Venus to draw its pentagonal pattern around Earth.
3168	2^5 x 3^2 x 11. Canonical num. Factors add to 6660.
3600	The square of 60. Seconds in an hour or degree.
3960	Radius of Earth in miles.
5040	7! = 1 x 2 x 3 x 4 x 5 x 6 x 7 = 7 x 8 x 9 x 10. Combined radii of Earth and Moon.
5913	1! + 2! + 3! + 4! + 5! + 6! + 7!.
7140	Largest triangular and tetrahedral num.
7200	Mayan Katun, or 20 Tuns of 360 days.
7920	Diameter of Earth in miles. = 720 x 11.
8128	The fourth perfect num, sum of its factors.
10000	A myriad.
20736	12 x 12 x 12 x 12.
25770	Current value for precession (seems to be slowing, suggesting the Sun forms a binary system with Sirius).
25920	12 x 2160. Years in the ancient western count for the precessional cycle of astrological ages.
26000	Mayan precessional figure.
31680	Perimeter of a square drawn around earth, in miles.
40320	8! = 1 x 2 x 3 x 4 x 5 x 6 x 7 x 8.
45045	The first triangular, pentagonal and hexagonal num.
86400	Num of seconds in a day.
108000	One season of a Kali Yuga.
142857	The repeating part of all divisions by seven.
144000	Days in a Mayan Baktun of 20 Katuns..
248832	12^5.
362880	9!, also = 2! x 3! x 3! x 7!
365242	Days in 1000 years. Num of feet in one degree of arc at the equator.
432000	The Hindu final and corrupt Kali Yuga period, in years.
864000	The Hindu third phase of creation, the semi-corrupt dwapara yuga, in years.
3628800	10!, also 6! x 7!, or 3! x 5! x 7!
1296000	The Hindu secondary Treta Yuga period, in years. = 3 x 432000.
1728000	The Hindu initiatory and highly spiritual Satya Yuga period, in years. = 4 x 432000.
1872000	Years in the Mayan long count (ends Dec 2012).
4320000	The Hindu Mahayuga, a complete cycle of Yugas, a Buddhist Kalpa.
39916800	11!, also 5040 x 7920.

FURTHER NUMBERS

	Triangular	Square	Pentagonal	Centred Triangular	Centred Square	Centred Pentagonal	Rectangular	Tetrahedral	Octahedral	Cubic	Centred Cube	Square Pyramidal	Fibonacci	Lucas
1	1	1	1	1	1	1	1	1	1	1	1	1	1	1
2	3	4	5	4	5	5	2	4	6	8	9	5	1	3
3	6	9	12	10	13	13	6	10	19	27	35	14	2	4
4	10	16	22	19	25	25	12	20	44	64	91	30	3	7
5	15	25	35	31	41	41	20	35	85	125	189	55	5	11
6	21	36	51	46	61	61	30	56	146	216	341	91	8	18
7	28	49	70	64	85	85	42	84	231	343	559	140	13	29
8	36	64	92	85	113	113	56	120	344	512	855	204	21	47
9	45	81	117	109	145	145	72	165	489	729	1241	285	34	76
10	55	100	145	136	181	181	90	220	670	1000	1729	385	55	123
11	66	121	176	166	221	221	110	286	891	1331	2331	506	89	199
12	78	144	210	199	265	265	132	364	1156	1728	3059	650	144	322
13	91	169	247	235	313	313	156	455	1469	2197	3925	819	233	521
14	105	196	287	274	365	365	182	560	1834	2744	4941	1015	377	843
15	120	225	330	316	421	421	210	680	2255	3375	6119	1240	610	1364
16	136	256	376	361	481	481	240	816	2736	4096	7471	1496	987	2207
17	153	289	425	409	545	545	272	969	3281	4913	9009	1785	1597	3571
18	171	324	477	460	613	613	306	1140	3894	5832	10745	2109	2584	5778
19	190	361	532	514	685	685	342	1330	4579	6859	12691	2470	4181	9349
20	210	400	590	571	761	761	380	1540	5340	8000	14859	2870	6765	15127
21	231	441	651	631	841	841	420	1771	6181	9261	17261	3311	10946	24476
22	253	484	715	694	925	925	462	2024	7106	10648	19909	3795	17711	39603
23	276	529	782	760	1013	1013	506	2300	8119	12167	22815	4324	28657	64079
24	300	576	852	829	1105	1105	552	2600	9224	13824	25991	4900	46368	103682
25	325	625	925	901	1201	1201	600	2925	10425	15625	29449	5525	75025	167761
26	351	676	1001	976	1301	1301	650	3276	11726	17576	33201	6201	121393	271443
27	378	729	1080	1054	1405	1405	702	3654	13131	19683	37259	6930	196418	439204
28	406	784	1162	1135	1513	1513	756	4060	14644	21952	41635	7714	317811	710647
29	435	841	1247	1219	1625	1625	812	4495	16269	24389	46341	8555	514229	1149851
30	465	900	1335	1306	1741	1741	870	4960	18010	27000	51389	9455	832040	1860498
21	496	961	1426	1396	1861	1861	930	5456	19871	29791	56791	10416	1346269	3010349
32	528	1024	1520	1489	1985	1985	992	5984	21856	32768	62559	11440	2178309	4870847
33	561	1089	1617	1585	2113	2113	1056	6545	23969	35937	68705	12529	3524578	7881196
34	595	1156	1717	1684	2245	2245	1122	7140	26214	39304	75241	13685	5702887	12752043
35	630	1225	1820	1786	2381	2381	1190	7770	28595	42875	82179	14910	9227465	20653239
36	666	1296	1926	1891	2521	2521	1260	8436	31116	46656	89531	16206	14930352	33385282

Primes 2 3 5 7 11 13 17 19 23 29 31 37 43 47 53 59 61 67 71 73 79 83 89 97 101 103 107 109 113 127 131 137 139 149 151 157 163 167 173 179 181 191 193 197 199 211 223 227 229 233 239 241 251 257 263 269 271 277 281 283 293 307 311 313 317 331 337 347 349 353 359 367 373 379 383 389 397 401 409 419 421 431 433 439 443 449 457 461 463 467 479 487 491 499 503 509 521 523 541 547 557 563 569 571 577 587 593 599 601 607 613 617 619 631 641 643 647 653 659 661 673 677 683 691 701 709 719 727 733 739 743 751 757 761 769 773 787 797 809 811 821 823 827 829 839 853 857 859 863 877 881 883 887 907 911 919 929 937 941 947 953 967 971 977 983 991 997 1009